PUTTING CUSTOMERS FIRST

**Putting Customers First: Re-envisioning Our Approach
to Transportation Planning
Volume Three**

May 2023

ISBN: 978-1-934276-52-5

Pacific Research Institute
P.O. Box 60485
Pasadena, CA 91116

www.pacificresearch.org

Nothing contained in this report is to be construed as necessarily reflecting the views of the Pacific Research Institute or as an attempt to thwart or aid the passage of any legislation. The views expressed remain solely the author's. They are not endorsed by any of the author's past or present affiliations.

PUTTING CUSTOMERS FIRST
RE-ENVISIONING OUR APPROACH
TO TRANSPORTATION PLANNING

By Steven Greenhut

VOLUME THREE

PR PACIFIC
RESEARCH
INSTITUTE

Giving the Public What the Planners Want

One need only spend a little time on a transit-oriented so-cial-media page or reading the thoughts of urban-focused writers to detect a certain disdain toward the automobile, sub-urbia and the construction of road and freeway lanes. Such at-titudes are not outliers, as any quick search of New Urbanist and pro-transit literature will reveal.[1] It's quickly apparent that many transit advocates are more about transforming the driving public's behavior than figuring out how to effi-ciently move people around within our current constraints.

"What driving really means for America is a rather tragic tale that allows most people to entirely escape the comments and connections – weak and strong – that occur in public space of the street," writes *MinnPost* columnist Bill Lindeke in a piece head-lined, "Why driving is bad for America."[2] In his view, simple commutes amount to "a Darwinian struggle for asphalt, view-ing our neighbors as nothing more than a relentless barrage of competitors for space and speed." Such hyperbole is not atypical.

That sounds like a terrifying scene from the dystopian movie "Road Warrior," but doesn't jibe with my daily experiences tooling around rural, suburban and city roads. We all run across reckless and distracted drivers, but I'm generally impressed by the degree to which drivers follow the rules and yield to one another. We drive to our destinations, but that doesn't stop us from making human connections once we arrive. Driving can be frustrating and isolating, but it's not particularly Darwinian.

The latest New Urbanist salvos feature diatribes against pickup trucks given that they make large targets for those troubled by our road dependence. Pickups are among the most popular vehicles on the road, with Ford's F150 the best-selling "car" in America. Critics are no doubt correct that most of their drivers use them as family transport rather than working vehicles. So what? They hardly amount to an "obnoxious assertion of dominance and division," as *Globe and Mail* columnist Marcus Gee asserted in a column in the Canadian newspaper last year.[3] This is part of a virtue-signaling process that depicts driving and freeway construction as an environmental scourge.

Even in the most environmentally friendly parts of the country, the public strongly supports efforts to reduce traffic congestion via highway expansions. The Oregon Department of Transportation recently conducted a survey that showed 86 percent of Portland-area respondents are supportive of efforts to address congestion problems along Interstate 5's Rose Corridor, yet a group called "No More Freeways" railed against ODOT's "disastrous, polluting, billion-dollar freeway expansions."[4]

One Facebook/webpage group of disgruntled transit advocates is not indicative of public sentiment, but similar – albeit more high-minded – critiques of the automobile are found throughout academia. And academic studies bolster public policies. "Auto-restraint policies often need to be introduced in parallel with

Transit Oriented Development (TOD) to off-set the hidden subsidies that promote automobility," writes Robert Cervero, director of the University of California Transportation Center.[5]

Auto-restraints aren't a reference to child-car seats or seatbelts, but to a set of policies that include bans on cars in central cities. They also include, "controls on the number of parking spaces, their spatial distribution, parking costs, parking time limits, residential parking permits, taxes, provision of employee parking, and levels of policy enforcement," according to one *Transportation Research Record* report.[6] Some of these policies might make sense in specific situations, but their goal is to limit our automobile usage and prod us into transit – not help us get around more efficiently.[7]

Politicians, of course, like to jump on that car-scolding bandwagon, especially in California where battling climate change is a top legislative and regulatory priority. This often means proposing policies that attempt to increase costs and regulatory impediments on driving. In recent years, Gov. Gavin Newsom announced a ban on the sale of new internal-combustion vehicles by 2030.[8] That would mandate a shift primarily to electric vehicles rather than transit, but the policy could have a vast impact on how Californians move around given the (for now) higher prices and limits of EVs.

But California policymakers who presumably rely on automobiles themselves, have for years been taking aim at the evils of our car dependence – even though our largest metropolitan area (Los Angeles) is a product of post-war suburban-style development patterns. In 2006, then-Attorney General Bill Lockyer filed "suit against the Big Six auto companies alleg(ing) that because vehicle exhaust contributes to global warming, the companies should be held financially liable for everything from wildfires to a bad ski season," the *Los Angeles Times* reported.[9] That was the first of a long-running campaign by state officials who like to prattle about the "unsustainability" of cars.

Just to be clear, this booklet and the Free Cities Center are not about promoting car usage per se. We recognize that many transit advocates raise valid points and promote some reasonable policies. One such policy – reducing mandatory parking minimums for new construction projects – is a sensible market-based idea that allows developers rather than planners to decide how much parking a project might need. But Free Cities is about finding better ways to increase the public's mobility within those cities and metro areas. Most Americans rely on their cars, so policymakers ought to focus more on building effective alternatives – and less on berating us for our pickup-truck preferences.

A September 2021 article by Gabby Birenbaum in *Vox* epitomizes the attitude that we, as practical transportation advocates, often face. Titled, "How to end the American obsession with driving," the article draws on her personal experience: "When I lived in Madrid, I could walk or take transit practically everywhere without ever crossing a highway that had no pedestrian infrastructure. I would take 30-minute walks home in the middle of the night from clubs, when the Metro was not running. Even in the dark, there were no crossings where I was unprotected as a pedestrian."[10]

For some perspective, Madrid has a population density of 14,000 people per square mile.[11] That's lower than the population density of San Francisco (18,790), but much higher than the density of Los Angeles (8,485), San Jose (5,812), Fresno (4,849) or Seattle (9,248).[12] Most Westerners live in suburban areas. The population density of metropolitan Portland, which imposed an urban-growth boundary to promote densification, is a mere 364 per square mile (5,025 within the city). Obviously, transit makes sense in densely packed areas, but most of us don't live in those places. We're not really "obsessed" with driving, but driving is the most practical choice for most of us.

The big question: Are urban planners and policymakers trying to help people get to their destinations or incentivize us to move into big cities? In my view, a transportation policy that first requires the total re-ordering of urban and suburban design is not so much a transportation policy as a land-use policy. It prioritizes social engineering over civil engineering. Our planning regimen can and perhaps should evolve over time, but in the meantime a proper transportation approach should help Americans get around within the communities they now live while loosening up land-use regulations so that communities can adapt in a natural, bottom-up manner.

Birenbaum quoted one telling tweet: "Americans only love the college experience because it's the only time in their lives they live in walkable communities."[13] That conforms to my cynical theory that many urban planners spent their college years in a big city (or spent a few months touring Europe) and now want to impose that preference on everybody else. I loved my experience at George Washington University in downtown Washington, D.C. Like many other young urbanites, my wife and I hightailed it to the suburbs for affordability, schooling, safety and space reasons upon the birth of our first child. Nostalgia is not the proper goal of planning, especially in a democratic society.

Unfortunately, policymakers across the country – but especially in California, Oregon and Washington – are immersed in the anti-driving, pro-density, transit-oriented thinking that I detailed above. This becomes obvious once one starts reading planning documents from the U.S. Department of Transportation, state transportation agencies and regional and local planning agencies. In them, one finds little attention to customer-oriented concerns (safety, scheduling, comfort, convenience) and a lot of attention to greenhouse gases and social equity concerns.

As an example, the California Department of Transportation in 2021 released its *California Transportation Plan 2050* – a blueprint for the state's transportation investments in the coming decades. This is not from a purely transit agency, but the state's main freeway-building agency (although it does play a key role in transit). This is from its executive summary:

> (T)ransportation does far more than connect people and goods to their destinations; it plays a central role in our economic opportunities, cost of living, environmental quality, health, and quality of life. Our transportation system also plays a vital role in increasing resilience to climate change, while helping bring down carbon emissions that lead to future climate impacts. … Over the past two and a half years, hundreds of Californians … have come together to lay out their vision for a transportation system that reflects our collective values as a state. They imagine a safe, resilient and universally accessible transportation system that

supports vibrant communities, advances racial and economic justice, and improves public and environmental health. … This plan seeks to advance racial and economic justice by redirecting resources to marginalized communities; better connecting individuals to jobs, health care, education, and other opportunities; improving environmental justice; and amplifying the voices of those who have been historically excluded from the transportation decision-making process.[14]

Certainly, any public planning process must legitimately address environmental and social-justice issues, but the lengthy document offers almost no discussion of the nuts-and-bolts concerns of California drivers – the people who transit advocates presumably need to lure out of their cars. The document gives short shrift to those typical day-to-day concerns from people who simply are trying to get to school, jobs, shopping centers and doctors' appointments. The plan's main identified challenges focus on improving public health, adapting to climate change, reducing greenhouse gas emissions, reducing vehicle miles travelled, advancing racial justice, closing the wealth gap, addressing the housing shortage and navigating the impacts of emerging technologies.

The latter point is fascinating, as Caltrans worries that new technologies – ridesharing services, dock-less bikes and scooters, drones and 5G internet—"could increase auto travel, exacerbate inefficient land use, and pose risks to our safety and privacy."[15] Most of us who are devoted to improving mobility view these innovations as benefits. There's no reason for the agency to view them as a threat. If urban dwellers take more Uber rides (something that's greatly improved my elderly mom's ability to leave her apartment, for instance), or zip to work on a bike or scooter, or work from home thanks to improved internet service, doesn't that help solve real-world transportation problems? Doesn't it help the environment, reduce traffic and improve people's lives?

Sadly, even groups that rely on public transportation often seem focused on the wrong piece of the puzzle. For instance, the Bus Riders Union, a group that advocates for improved bus mobility in Los Angeles, addresses the transit issue from a civil rights perspective rather than a consumer-oriented one. BRU does at least prioritize "ridership needs," but its literature includes critiques of the city's auto dependency and air pollution.[16] It sees transit as a means for community revitalization, improved public health and energy efficiency. Better transit can indeed help the economy and provide other public benefits as an aside, but it's primarily about getting people to their destinations.

The group promotes the concept of "free" public transportation.[17] Unfortunately, when something is free – or complimentary, as my libertarian colleagues will say – people tend not to value it very much.[18] It distorts supply and demand. Los Angeles did in fact eliminate all subway fees during the COVID-19 pandemic. That policy "turned the system into a mobile homeless shelter, psychiatric ward, drug den and armed free-for-all" and "significantly deterred former users who say crime and disorder are keeping them off the buses and trains," as Free Cities Center writer Kenneth Schrupp noted in a column.[19]

If transit planners are serious about luring people onto buses and trains, they need to start viewing those systems primarily as transportation conveyances and not civil-rights and environmental instruments. If they want to help car-dependent Westerners seek out alternatives when appropriate, they need to spend less time haranguing drivers and more time reforming transit systems (and not just by seeking more public funding) so they appeal to potential riders. They need to make these systems better for the small subset of residents who rely on them.

Americans are Voting with their Feet (and their Cars)

American planners and public transportation agencies are unquestionably committed to boosting transit ridership and reducing car mileage, yet they haven't grappled with reality. Even before the pandemic, transit ridership has been falling. They need to look at the data, talk with riders and former riders and try to understand the ridership freefall. They need to think more like private executives confronting a collapse in business and less like community activists, bureaucrats, politicians, academics and planners. That might entail an impossible shift in thinking, but it's necessary.

Bloomberg's Jonathan English puts the data in historical perspective: "One hundred years ago, the United States had a public transportation system that was the envy of the world. Today, outside a few major urban centers, it is barely on life support. Even in New York City, subway ridership is well below its 1946 peak. Annual per capita transit trips in the U.S. plummeted from 115.8 in 1950 to 36.1 in 1970, where they have roughly remained since, even as population has grown."[20]

He notes that the U.S. experience differs from most of the developed world – but the fall can't be blamed on cars, but on agencies' failure to provide better local service. All government agencies are inefficient and wasteful, but ours have been particularly subservient to the demands of public-employee unions and tied to a bureaucratic model that neglects the customer and prioritizes highfalutin social-change goals.[21] One need only look at other developed Western nations to realize that the United States has made a particular mess of its transit systems.

"Canada, like its European and Asian counterparts, has built systems that cater to riders, not to special interest groups," summarizes economist William L. Anderson, in a February 2023 Free Cities Center article. "Unlike the 'park-and-ride' system in U.S. cities, Toronto provides extensive bus services in neighborhoods that provide access to the commuter rail systems, providing clean, comfortable surroundings. European systems also make themselves commuter-friendly and reliable."[22] Later in this book, I'll address ways to improve that situation, primarily by enlisting the efforts of the private sector, but for now let's grapple with the numbers.

Many transit activists in part blame the transit ridership freefall on the unique COVID-19 situation. The stay-at-home orders kept people locked down in their homes. Urban dwellers feared that riding subways and buses would spread the virus. Large numbers of Americans shifted toward virtual work and even moved out of cities given that they could work at home from remote locations. Even with the pandemic over, it's unlikely urban life will completely return to the pre-COVID status quo. According to federal data, the number of Americans who worked from home increased from 9 million to 27.6 million between 2019 and 2021. The *Wall Street Journal* noted that bigger cities such as San Francisco and Seattle saw the largest increases in remote work. It also noted that transit ridership fell by more than half over that timeframe.[23]

Published in the midst of the pandemic, a *Politico* article noted that transit systems faced a worldwide "reckoning," as agencies faced plummeting ridership and revenue.[24] Agencies did eventually receive large infusions of federal cash and ridership has increased somewhat since then, but it's been a slow recovery. NPR explained in September 2022 that a "recent report by S&P Global Ratings indicates that transit ridership, especially on trains into downtown areas, will remain down for years with only a 75 percent ridership recovery predicted by the end of 2025."[25]

Focusing on COVID, however, will only divert rail and bus authorities from the long-term trends. The regional planning agency known as the Southern California Association of Governments (SCAG) published a remarkably hardheaded analysis of transit trends in 2018. It found that Southern California had "invested heavily in public transportation" since the early 1990s, including the construction of 530 miles of commuter rail and 100 miles of light and heavy rail in Los Angeles County. Yet the investments "have not been matched by increases in transit ridership."[26] Transit ridership's peak occurred in 1985 – before most of these projects were on the drawing boards.

Actually, "not matched by increases" is a nice way of saying "precipitous declines." The report found that between 2012 and

2016 the six-county SCAG region, with more than 19-million people, saw 72-million fewer transit rides annually over that four-year period and that the decline affects all modes of transit. Even more telling, SCAG reported that while the average resident of the region made 35 transit trips annually but the median resident made no – as in zero – transit trips in a given year. In reality, a tiny number of residents take the preponderance of transit trips (mostly in Los Angeles) and that transit ridership is concentrated in 1.4-percent of the region's census tracts, per its own data.[27]

Transit certainly can help move some people around in some places, but policymakers need to focus their attention on improving service in those neighborhoods where it makes the most sense and building commuter systems that might make sense to others during commute times – rather than worrying so much about widespread car dependence. A good starting point: grappling with why fewer people are hopping on buses and trains for their commutes. A November 2022 survey by the Los Angeles Metropolitan Transit Authority (LA Metro) found that women riders in particular had ditched its mass-transit offerings. Female ridership dropped below its rate three years earlier.[28]

One transit organizer interviewed by the *Los Angeles Times* "said it's hard to pinpoint one reason for decreased female ridership, but noted the pandemic is still affecting many women, who are struggling financially as they are unable to return to the jobs they held before the pandemic."[29] Actually, it's not that hard to pinpoint the top reason. Fortunately, the *Times* seemed familiar with Occam's razor – the idea that the simplest explanation usually is the most likely one. In this case, the newspaper

interviewed former riders and agency officials who acknowl-
edged that a lack of safety and cleanliness likely is driving the
reduction. Women in particular – and not surprisingly – are
fearful of increased crime.

Falling ridership is nothing new and has a wide range of
causes. Pointing to a dramatic overall drop in transit ridership in 31 of 35 U.S. cities, transit planner Jarrett Walker told
The Washington Post that the drop off "needs to be considered
an emergency." He viewed it as a threat to "the livelihood, the
viability, the livability and the economy of a city."[30] The U.S.
Department of Transportation released this data in March 2018
– well before anyone had heard of the coronavirus. The article
concluded that the losses largely stemmed from reliability issues.
Policymakers might talk about reducing global emissions, but
individual riders worry about bread-and-butter issues such as a
bus showing up on time.

The libertarian Cato Institute's Randal O'Toole explained
in 2020 that transit ridership had fallen 40 percent in the nation's
top 50 metropolitan areas in 2018 – and that the raw number of
people taking transit fell by 146,000 between 2015 and 2018
– even as the nation added 6.3 million jobs. "These declines
have taken place in spite of huge increases in spending on public
transit," he wrote, including an annual increase of 7.4 percent in
2018 alone.[31] Against this reality, throwing more money at the
problem is unlikely to achieve planners' desired results.

Transit remains dominant in the New York City area, he
added, but it's an outlier. Even in the San Francisco Bay Area,
Seattle and Chicago, it only accounts for a dwindling amount of
metro-area commutes (ranging from 10 percent to 18 percent).

I don't agree with his conclusion that transit is "the urban parasite," but its financing needs to be dispensed in ways that help actual people get around their regions rather than viewed as a means to change our habits. Transit is part of the mix, but the goal should be to make it better and more useful for those who want to use it.

Debates about freeways and transit ultimately lead to priorities about how to spend limited taxpayer dollars. Transit advocates argue that automobiles are highly subsidized by the federal government, so it's a matter of misplaced priorities to spend the bulk of our transportation dollars on roads and freeways rather than mass transit. In their view, public agencies have to make a choice, so it's unfair to continue choosing car-oriented approaches – as the nation has largely done since the dawn of the automobile era. Transit backers claim that every form of transportation is subsidized, so why not subsidize their preference? There's much to unpack in this simple question.

On one hand, most Americans – the vast majority, actually – rely on their cars, so car advocates would suggest that government dollars ought to flow toward improving the transportation systems that Americans use rather than the ones that serve a fraction of the population. On the other hand, transit advocates argue that perhaps more Americans would choose transit if transit agencies had the necessary funds to build out their lines to where Americans live. We can actually do both – fund transit where it makes sense and roads and freeways where they make sense. But before we address that choice, it's worth looking at which type of transportation receives the lion's share of subsidies.

Let's turn to O'Toole again, as he is a master of these road v. transit statistics. In a 2019 article in his *Anti-Planner* blog, O'Toole looks at the total amount of general-fund dollars (from the feds, states and local governments) spent on highways and roads and then subtracts the amount of money that agencies divert from those programs to mass transit projects.[32] That's a staple of government, by the way. Voters might pass, say, an infrastructure bond that promises to fund the car-oriented projects they prefer – but a look at the fine print reveals that a large portion of that "road" funding goes to transit and bike lanes.

Most highway funding operates like a user fee, in that the gasoline tax and vehicle-registration fees fund the construction and maintenance of freeways and Interstate highways. But governments divert a significant portion of these fees paid by drivers to transit, bike lanes and environmental-related projects. He concluded that in 2017 local, state and federal governments collected $86.1 billion in highway user fees, of which $35 billion was diverted to non-highway uses. Based on miles traveled, all governments, he concluded, subsidize drivers by 0.8 cents a passenger mile – with most of those subsidies coming from property taxes that pay for local roads and streets given that our Interstate highway system largely pays its own way thanks to those user fees.[33]

Regarding transit, he subtracted the fares that riders pay and then calculated the resulting public subsidy. The final figure is a subsidy of 91.9 cents per passenger mile. Of the various types of transit, streetcars and light rail receive the most taxpayer subsidies, and commuter and heavy rail the least. Buses are somewhere in between.[34] One might argue that the government *should* subsidize transit for basic equity, intracity congestion and environmental reasons, but that's a matter of preference rather than math.

To get around these lopsided numbers, transit cheerleaders will argue that car transportation does not include a variety of "hidden" externalities relating to pollution, social equity and healthcare costs from accidents. There is some truth there (although rail and buses would impose similar costs if it were more widespread), but transit advocates wildly inflate those "externalities." It's really just an effort to divert attention from the realities of government finance. If one assesses driving with indeterminate costs related to climate change, then it's a rigged formula that will always lead to the desired conclusion (more transit funding!).[35] As with all government-dominated expenditures, we ought to know as accurately as possible where the money is going as we attempt to use resources effectively.

The key math takeaway is clear: Transit receives far more subsidies than driving, yet Americans still are voting with their cars.

So Why are Americans Shrugging at Transit?

Although I've always enjoyed cars and the sense of freedom and mobility they offer, I never had any objection to using public transportation. In my mind, they're different tools that serve different functions. Growing up in the suburbs, I relied on my car to get to most destinations, but I never hesitated to take the commuter train into downtown Philadelphia. During Christmas shopping season, my entire family would board the train and head to Center City. It beat parking downtown and was an annual holiday tradition. I'd take the Amtrak to get to college in Washington, D.C., where owning a car was an expensive annoyance during those years. In these cases, transit made practical and economic sense to me as a transportation consumer.

I even took the bus to work when I lived in Des Moines, which was a challenge during that city's frequent sub-zero temperatures. Nevertheless, the economics of an $11.50 a month bus pass fit my budget at the time much better than buying another automobile. In Southern California, transit was an ordeal. I recall reading one *Orange County Register* column where the reporter detailed the hours-long bus ordeal of getting from a

South Orange County suburb to downtown Los Angeles, 38 miles away. Transit didn't fit my suburb-to-suburb commute and I never even tried taking it. In the Sacramento area, I tried a couple of times to take the RT light-rail line, but it took far longer (and cost more, when parking at one end and a taxi at the other were considered) to get to my destination than just driving. I might sometimes take the RT if it went to the airport or the Amtrak to San Francisco if it didn't force me to de-board in Oakland and hop on a bus. But there I go again, thinking like a consumer.

I share those mundane observations because that's how customers think. I'm not completing some carbon-footprint calculation before deciding how to get to work or the store. I don't care which stakeholders' voices were – or weren't – amplified during the process of determining the proper rail or bus route. I am uninterested in the demands of striking transit workers. It's not that I don't care about environmental issues or social equity or wage concerns, but I simply am trying to get to where I'm going – and will choose the method that makes the most sense. Certainly, car ownership is expensive, so I'm open to reducing those costs – but only if the alternative is safe, reliable and convenient. And there's nothing wrong with putting a priority on my time and comfort.

I referred earlier to English's piece about falling transit ridership.[36] Although a transit advocate, he doesn't blame cars or a lack of state or federal transit funding. Instead, he points to a very simple and obvious problem: local transit agencies aren't providing adequate service, which creates a vicious cycle. As the population shifted to the suburbs, transit agencies lost ridership and cut back their service to shore up their inflexible budgets. "The only way to reverse the vicious cycle in the U.S. is by providing better service up front," he added. These agencies have championed high-profile marquee projects such as light-rail lines, he continued, but they often have "little connecting bus service to provide access to people not within walking distance of their shops." I've seen that myself, as the RT's terminus lands me in a community college parking lot in the middle of nowhere.

When I covered Orange County's failed attempt to build a billion-dollar rail line in the early 2000s, bus riders were furious because the proposal prioritized luring new riders at the expense of existing transit users by reworking the bus schedules to accommodate rail.[37] Nearly 20 years later, the Orange County Transportation Authority (OCTA) is proposing a $509-million streetcar project in downtown Santa Ana – labeled the "Train to Hell" by downtown merchants who are concerned about the impact of construction on their businesses and potential gentrification.[38] The former concern is typical with any major construction project, but the latter touches on rail planners' emphasis on cool niche rail projects that aren't going to appeal to many people. This raises a dilemma.

There's a certain logic to building a system that might appeal to car-dependent residents rather than simply catering to the existing, mostly lower-income clientele. For instance, *Vox*'s Joseph Stromberg complains that, essentially, U.S. cities view their transit systems as a form of welfare. Up until the 1950s, he noted that many private companies operated bus systems and streetcars, but they were excruciatingly slow and their operators were locked into municipal contracts that limited fares. "When cities took over these companies … it was with the notion that they'd maintain these systems as a sort of welfare service – mostly for people who couldn't afford to drive," he added.[39]

That mentality has persisted, with bus accessibility and fare issues treated as civil rights issues. Note my reference earlier to LA's Bus Riders Union earlier. Stromberg argues that the low fares limit the systems' ability to offer more frequent service. That then limits the willingness of non-poor people to ride. In Europe and even Canada, by contrast, urban transit systems "have higher fares and more frequent service." That reinforces my point that more people might try a bus or rail if the service wasn't bad – even if they had to pay a little more to get it.[40] The focus on the equity aspects of urban transit instead prioritize low-cost or even "free" riding on substandard systems, he added.

That Orange County experience also points to the other side of the dilemma. Creating systems designed to appeal to commuters – most of whom will not take transit, anyway – will, in a world of scarce resources, lead to a de-emphasis on the bus routes relied upon by existing riders. In the public sector, everything is about divvying up a limited taxpayer pie, whereas in the private sector new voluntary investments create a growing set of choices and opportunity. There's no simple answer, but it's clear that government bureaucracies aren't particularly adept at adjusting their offerings to meet consumer demand. That's why private and privatized solutions, detailed later, offer the best hope. Nevertheless, public agencies certainly have the wherewithal to deal with some basic problems.

Before investing heavily in boutique lines, transit agencies should get their basic bus services into order. That means increasing route frequency and reliability, providing clean buses and, most significantly, assuring riders' safety. A recent analysis of the Bay Area Rapid Transit (BART) system, which began offering rail service in 1972, shows that it has been plagued with delays.[41]

Customer satisfaction levels keep falling according to its owner ridership surveys and it continues to face a ridership freefall. Recent news stories suggest that one major problem is a growing violent crime problem on its subways. BART's experiences are not outliers, but exemplify transit problems nationwide.

In August 2022, a woman was "sitting down on board a train car when a man came up behind her and put his hands inside her shirt," the *East Bay Times* reported. "She told him to stop and pulled away, after which he allegedly punched her multiple times in the face and held her against her will."[42] BART claims that it is dealing with such troubling incidents, but the long-term statistics are not encouraging. In 2019, the Alameda County Civil Grand Jury released a report showing robberies had increased 128 percent over four years and that aggravated assaults were up 83 percent.[43] Crime fell on the system following reduced COVID ridership. It is up again, according to recent reports.

One San Francisco business is offering self-defense classes specifically targeted to transit riders, which might offer useful strategies for riders.[44] But publicity about that service might only exacerbate public concerns. If transit officials want to boost ridership, they must, at a minimum, offer a reliably safe riding experience. Urban writer Ed West, on his Substack page, emphasized that latter point – in a rebuttal to those who keep blaming cars for a decline not just in transit but urban life in general. As he noted, "You can't have cities without civility."[45] And you cannot have civility amid a crime plague. Nor can we have a rational debate about improving transit ridership and our transportation systems if the loudest voices prefer car hectoring to problem solving.

Another problem, from my personal experience, also is obvious. Riding transit is often unpleasant and even bleak. Sure, driving can be unpleasant, too, but it's a different sort of unpleasant. The last time I rode the RT, two homeless people were involved in a romantic encounter that I'll never be able to un-see. I remember the time taking a D.C. Metro bus when a homeless man peed on the floor, and the rest of us raised our feet every time the bus took a turn. Yuck. The D.C. transit cops made some high-profile arrests of people who committed the horrific crime of drinking coffee or eating a sandwich on the subway car. When I take the Washington State ferry system, by contrast, it's pleasurable.

The ferries have cafes where we can buy a latte or muffin. They have clean restrooms and comfortable seats. Granted, riding across the Puget Sound or Salish Sea is a blast for scenic reasons that can't be replicated in Sacramento or Washington, D.C., but perhaps there are some lessons here for transit operators.

Congress and state legislatures (not to mention voters, via myriad transportation bonds) have directed increasing windfalls in the direction of mass-transit systems. "President Biden and the U.S. Department of Transportation's Federal Transit Administration (FTA) today announced a more than $20 billion investment in American transit, thanks to the Bipartisan Infrastructure Law," the administration announced in April

2022. "The funding levels, detailed by FTA in apportionment tables for each of 30 programs for Fiscal Year 2022, will provide 58 percent more funding, enabling transit agencies to modernize and expand services for residents in communities large and small."[46] At least it's on record – transit funding continues to soar.

In February 2023, California Gov. Gavin Newsom announced "an award of more than $2.5 billion to 16 ongoing public transportation projects in the first wave of a historic infusion of state funding to expand transit and passenger rail service throughout the state, helping to cut planet-warming pollution."[47] With the administration's focus on climate change, such spending will continue to grow. Yet much of this money passes through to local transit agencies, which always find themselves financially strapped.

Part of that conundrum involves the nature of government agencies, which seem immune to dollar stretching. I've yet to find any agency or official who says, "Yes, we have plenty of money to meet our needs." Even with state and federal dollars, these agencies could get more bang for the buck if they spent their resources with some restraint. BART, for instance, has train operators who receive total-compensation packages of $259,000. One BART janitor earned $271,000 in 2015.[48] One need only look at the Transparent California database to see the kind of compensation received by California transit officials.[49] Your. Mind. Will. Be. Blown. If an agency spends that kind of money on salaries, it obviously has less money to spend in ways that benefit riders.

Union contracts not only drive up the costs of operating these transit systems, but they leave riders at the mercy of routine strikes and work slowdowns. Transit advocates often point to Europe as a model, but as of this writing French union workers had shuttered buses and rail lines across the country as part of a strike over pension benefits and working conditions.[50] The more dependent we are on transit, the more susceptible we are to having our lives disrupted by labor disputes. The more dependent we become on transit, the more leverage that union activists will have.

Public-sector unions also remain an impediment to reform in every public agency. Public schools and police agencies cannot implement new, more-efficient procedures without incurring the wrath of their collective-bargaining units. The same dynamic takes place in transit agencies. During one bargaining dispute in Orange County, the transit authority wanted to hire more entry-level bus drivers and expand the number of bus lines – but older workers who dominated the bus-drivers' union preferred the money be spent in ways that benefitted retirees.[51]

This is baked into the operation of public bureaucracies, but that reality only makes transit ridership less enticing to would-be riders. Union costs and resistance to outsourcing, of course, also impede road and freeway improvements. In private industry, the customer generally comes first because without a strong customer base the enterprise falters. In government, not so much.

Grappling with Cars and Freeways

Conservatives had a field day in 2022 blasting legislation by then-Democratic Assembly member Cristina Garcia that would have outlawed the construction of new freeway lanes in urban neighborhoods and diverted the revenue to new environmentally friendly projects.[52] Assembly Bill 1778 would have "prohibit(ed) any state funds or personnel time from being used to fund or permit freeway projects in certain areas" based on indicators in the California Healthy Places Index, which ranks the environmental health of various neighborhoods.[53]

Garcia's central Los Angeles district isn't prime freeway-building territory, but the measure could have had a debilitating effect on other urban areas that are trying to deal with snarled traffic. "It is outrageous and feels criminal to use state resources to choke and displace communities like mine when the data and research clearly show that this practice is just another example of the systemic racism that is normalized in our policies and practices," Garcia said in her author statement.[54]

Garcia isn't entirely wrong that infrastructure projects often have targeted poorer communities. In my previous Free Cities Center book, *Back From Dystopia,* I detailed the way that

1950s-era urban planners obliterated many settled inner-city neighborhoods in a rush to build freeways that connected the growing suburbs to downtown business districts.[55] I've always preferred urban theorist Jane Jacobs' neighborhood-centric urban-planning approach to the one pioneered by New York's infamous Robert Moses – the architect of large-scale road and redevelopment projects.[56] The nation's highway building spree did destroy and divide many neighborhoods.

Yet in trying to undo a previous generation's road-construction harms, Garcia offered a plan that would create modern-day harms by limiting the state's ability to expand and improve a freeway system that people rely upon. As an aside, she failed to acknowledge that many freeways were built largely on vacant land – and surrounding communities have later become home to lower-income residents because those areas now have lower real estate values as freeway-adjacent locations have become less-appealing places to live. Distinctions make a difference.

The bill died in committee, but it is part of a broader movement to demolish existing freeways. The liberal *American Prospect* last year pointed to Biden administration grants that, as a Congress for the New Urbanism official explained, "will go out to different cities to explore what they can do with highways that cause environmental, social and economic damage around them."[57] Some cities have in fact bulldozed freeway sections and replaced them with mixed-use developments, parks and boulevards. That has its place at times (and some of these pedestrian-oriented projects are pretty cool), but hard-and-fast legislation will only make the task of improving road infrastructure that much harder.

New projects should indeed be sensitive to existing neighborhoods, but these ideologically driven approaches are, again, all about social aims rather than transportation goals. The brouhaha over Garcia's bill also concealed one important fact: California has largely stopped expanding its system of freeway infrastructure. In 2001, then-Gov. Gray Davis cut the ribbon at the opening of a 28-mile section of the Foothill Freeway in San Bernardino County, 50 miles east of Los Angeles.

"Standing atop eight lanes of grooved pavement and pristine yellow stripes in the kind of distant Los Angeles suburb made possible by endless highway construction, Gov. Gray Davis today dedicated the latest section of freeway to be built in California and declared that the project would be the last," *The New York Times* reported at the time.[58] "While the state will be spending much more money on transportation in coming years, Mr. Davis, a Democrat, said it would be mostly for mass transit like trains and buses."

That was 22 years ago and, as the above-quoted *California Transportation Plan 2050* shows, California has indeed been making good on Davis' promise.[59] In fact, the state hasn't significantly expanded its freeway capacity since that freeway expansion when the state had 5 million fewer people. It hadn't completed many expansions for years prior to that, either, which helps explain why the state's metro areas routinely top the charts of the most congested regions in the country. As transit ridership numbers show, these drivers are not shifting to alternative forms of transit in large enough numbers to make a noticeable difference. Quite the reverse.

Policymakers need to come to terms with the fact that most Americans rely on their cars, will continue to do so for the foreseeable future and that road-related infrastructure needs immediate attention if we're going to improve our mobility. Furthermore, cars remain the transportation of choice if we're serious about helping poor people escape poverty.[60]

In his study for the Free Cities Center, demographer Wendell Cox pointed to the "Marchetti Constant," which references the statistic that 60 percent of American workers commute less than 30 minutes each way to their jobs. No matter how metropolitan areas grow, most people choose to live within that reasonable commuting distance from their jobs. His basic point is transit generally takes much longer than driving and car ownership opens up a larger number of job opportunities – of great significance for lower-income earners.[61]

Cox also notes that only 12.8 percent of workers who live in poverty use transit to get to work compared to 72.7 percent who use cars. The bottom line: Improving the job prospects of lower-income workers means also improving the road infrastructure that the vast majority of them rely upon – especially in urban areas with fewer quick and reliable transit options. Many of the state's poorest metros, such as Fresno and Bakersfield, have the least viable transit systems.[62]

State leaders point to transit investments in the name of social equity, but most low-income workers drive their cars because it increases their ability to get to work opportunities – and to do so in a relatively timely manner. "This is *not* an argument for cars, but simply a recognition that cars better serve what many (including this author) consider to be the ultimate domestic public policy objectives – improving affluence and re-ducing poverty," Cox noted.[63]

Even liberal-oriented think tanks acknowledge this fact. Writing in the *Daily Beast*, Scott Beyer, editor of the Market Urbanism forum, points to a 2011 Brookings Institution study showing "in the 100 largest U.S. metro areas, only 22 percent of low- and middle-skill jobs were accessible by public transit in under 90 minutes."[64] A 2014 study by the Urban Institute found that "car owners were twice as likely as transit users to find jobs and four times likelier to retain them." This echoes "previous work by the Progressive Policy Institute arguing that car owner-ship plants the seeds of upward mobility," Beyer added.

Unfortunately, California and other Western states contin-ue to defund their highway systems under the idea that freeway building is a wasteful enterprise. Even when voters become fed up and raise their taxes to pay for expanded road infrastructure, they don't always get what they bargained for. Then-Gov. Jerry Brown in 2017 signed Senate Bill 1, which approved higher gasoline and diesel excise taxes and created a Transportation Improvement Fee levied on privately owned vehicles (based on estimated value). Brown and supporters appealed to the public's frustration at congestion.

"The deterioration of California's state and local streets and roads and state highway system has been widely documented.

Specifically, the state highways system is facing a $59 billion deferred maintenance backlog for road maintenance and repairs. The total shortfall for local streets and roads maintenance is approximately $7.3 billion annually," the Assembly bill analysis concluded.[65]

Californians often see road signs touting some SB1-funded project ("Your Tax Dollars At Work!"). Lawmakers even included a "lockbox" to assure the funds weren't raided for other programs.

The reality was a bit different. "Although SB 1 raised taxes with the promise that the money would be used to repair crumbling roads and bridges, about 30 percent of the revenue raised by the tax hike is designated for other transportation priorities, including public transit, bike lanes and walk paths," wrote Jon Coupal, president of the Howard Jarvis Taxpayers Association. "And the law includes not one reform to address the well-documented waste at the California Department of Transportation."[66]

One of the oddest spending priorities involved something known as Road Diets.[67] Many Californians, who were now paying an extra $5.4 billion in taxes, figured at least they would get some new roads and freeway lanes. Few of us were surprised to learn, as Coupal pointed out, that a portion of the funding went to bike lanes and environmental projects.[68] That's an accepted part of road spending these days, but many people were surprised that some of the money was going to actually *reduce* the number of road lanes to purposefully slow down traffic. That sounds literally unbelievable.

Sacramento embraced these diets with zeal and it became immediately obvious to those of us who commuted downtown that traffic along the main downtown streets that fed into the freeways had become a snarled mess. "A classic Road Diet typically involves converting an existing four-lane, undivided roadway segment to a three-lane segment consisting of two through lanes and a center, two-way left-turn lane," the Federal Highway

Administration explains, but such diets can apply broadly to other projects that reduce lanes and replace them with bike lanes and walkways.[69]

"Though the concept has won plaudits in many circles, it's also generating opposition from community groups who think the city's intentionally making it so miserable to drive that people will have no choice but to choose other ways to travel," according to an article for Rice University's Kinder Institute for Urban Research. The critics have a valid point, but the writer notes that, "even the federal government says the technique is effective."[70]

Effective at what? "Before-and-after studies of road diet projects have given the Federal Highway Administration and local transportation departments the confidence to declare it a cheap way to reduce vehicle collisions and make roads more bike and pedestrian friendly," the article continues. Well, certainly, if cities eliminate lanes and grind traffic to a halt, it almost certainly will lead to fewer collisions. Sacramento Mayor Darrell Steinberg said in a news report that, "the primary collision factor on the streets was unsafe speeds ... and one of the easiest and most cost-effective ways to reduce the speeds is to reduce the number of travel lanes."[71]

When some of us refer to "planned congestion" – apparent efforts by transit activists to increase congestion as a way to force us out of our cars – critics might view that as an overstatement. They agree that policymakers and bureaucrats might be misguided or incompetent, but surely none of them are purposefully trying to worsen traffic. Yet Road Diets are highly popular in city governments and have the federal government's seal of approval. They are – by their own definition – an attempt to reduce road lanes in a way that slows down traffic to achieve greater bike usage and safety. Isn't that *prima facie* evidence of a planned-congestion strategy?

The National Motorists Association offers a more sensible solution: "upgrade and improve the traffic handling capabilities of main thoroughfares" with infrastructure improvements, proper speed limits and synchronized traffic controls.[72] Road Diets are the product of ideologues and social engineers, whereas NMA's ideas stem from those who are trying to improve transportation. Whatever one's view, it's crazy that new tax money that promises to reduce congestion is purposefully used to increase it.

That focus on bizarre social engineering schemes by transportation planners makes me leery whenever they promote new ideas – even ones that sound reasonable on the surface. For instance, California officials are considering using a road-user fee based on vehicle miles traveled to replace fuel excise taxes.[73] The reason, of course, is that the growing number of electric vehicles aren't paying their share of road taxes because their drivers obviously aren't buying gasoline.[74]

Charging by the mile makes economic sense, especially from the market logic that people should pay for services based on the amount they use. The idea has potential problems, as it would punish the owners of fuel-efficient cars, who would have fewer incentives to reduce gasoline usage. The broader concern is whether California policymakers would actually replace the entire excise tax with the road-user charge or simply add the charge on top of existing excise taxes. I'm betting on the latter.

At the very least, a road-user tax at least represents a broader look at the transportation funding system. If planners want to improve their road and transit systems, they need to think out of the box in other ways, as well. In particular, it's time for transportation officials to embrace private-sector measures that could improve road and transit systems.

Private Solutions to Public Transportation Problems

When San Francisco was building its Transbay Transit Center, which is now the central bus terminal for the entire Bay Area, the project had generated controversy for being $300-million over budget in 2013. At the time, it was little more than a giant hole in the ground. Former San Francisco Mayor and Assembly Speaker Willie Brown raised eyebrows when he offered his forthright thoughts in his *San Francisco Chronicle* column:

> In the world of civic projects, the first budget is really just a down payment. If people knew the real cost from the start, nothing would ever be approved. The idea is to get going. Start digging a hole and make it so big, there's no alternative to coming up with the money to fill it in.[75]

I'd argue that such cynicism explains why the public often is reticent about supporting major infrastructure projects, whether they involve mass transit or anything else. We know that what Brown said is true – the promised price tag is always just a down payment. The projects rarely live up to the promises. Transbay advocates said it would be like a Grand Central Station for the West Coast, but the center has yet to become the promised hub for commuter trains.[76]

Pick any major infrastructure project and the template is the same. Boston's relatively successful (for a public project) Big Dig – a giant tunnel that rerouted Interstate 93 and mass-transit lines under Boston Harbor – opened nine years late. Following "tunnel leaks, epic traffic jams . . . (the) death of a motorist crushed by concrete ceiling panels and a price tag that soared from $2.6 billion to a staggering $14.8 billion, there's little appetite for celebration," the *Washington Post* noted in 2007.[77]

I was 29 years old when Americans settled in to watch game three of the 1989 World Series between the Oakland Athletics and the San Francisco Giants. We watched in horror as, just before game time, the Loma Prieta earthquake shook the region, causing 63 deaths, thousands of injuries and $6 billion in damage. It destroyed one 50-foot section of the Bay Bridge connecting Oakland and San Francisco. Caltrans replaced that section within a month, but it launched a process for a permanent fix that involved building a new eastern span of the bridge.[78]

Major projects take time, but the new span didn't open until 2013 – and was 2,500-percent (no typo) over budget.[79] Myriad studies show that 85 percent of major construction projects worldwide come in over budget – and usually significantly so.[80] Analysts point to a variety of obvious factors – rising materials costs, political disputes and planning delays – but often the problem is rather simple. "Far too often public funds are wasted because government officials believe they are playing with 'house money,'" wrote Joseph Szyliowicz in a 2015 article in *Quartz*.[81] They also are operating on slow-moving government timetables.

Whenever a major project is announced, public officials create project labor agreements to benefit union contractors and other cost-adding measures. Yet as Szyliowicz concluded, governments can reduce the overruns and problems by relying more on public-private partnerships that improve accountability and reduce risk. Some states are much better than others at harnessing the private sector and stretching their dollars.

The Reason Foundation regularly analyzes the cost-effectiveness of state highway-building programs. In its 2021 edition, it found that California spends nearly three times per mile more than Texas ($205,924 v. $75,153) in building roads and freeways. According to the group's standards, California also has worse pavement conditions and a larger number of deficient bridges. Perhaps California officials have paid too much attention to the Willie Brown strategy and not enough to the economics of accountability and competition.[82] The state could get more of everything – from freeway lanes to transit routes – if it spent its money more efficiently.

The California Department of Transportation often seems impervious to cutting unnecessary costs. The Legislative Analyst's Office in 2014 found that the agency's budget allowed it to be "overstaffed by about 3,500 full-time equivalents beginning in 2014-15 at a cost of more than $500 million."[83] Various unions, including those representing professional engineers, consistently fight outsourcing proposals to protect their members' jobs. During COVID, Caltrans finally eliminated those Bay Area bridge toll takers who ultimately slowed down drivers as they headed across the bridges. The agency didn't eliminate their jobs, however, but moved them to other parts of the department.[84] Such wastefulness reduces its investments in infrastructure that benefits residents.

Although some of the nation's original transit systems were developed and operated by private companies, it's unrealistic politically and practically to move toward a genuinely private transportation system on a large-scale basis. But Western states can embrace privatization, by which government entities issue construction and operation contracts that incentivize cost savings and service improvements. They can harness the forces of private innovation and turn over the operation of government infrastructure to private parties in a way that puts public concerns above bureaucratic and union ones.

"Privatization of airports has improved efficiency in Australia and the United Kingdom and has sped the advance of air traffic control technology in Canada," concluded a paper by the Brookings Institution's Clifford Winston. In another study, Winston explains that the results of privatization are mixed, but "a transparent, well-structured agreement in which the government sells assets to private firms could improve infrastructure performance and financing."[85]

Furthermore, the study concludes that policymakers can improve even government-run transportation systems by embracing privately developed technologies. It's already doing that to an extent. For example, the FasTrak transponders that drivers install on their cars had already rendered those toll takers largely obsolete even before COVID made that obvious. Too often, the study notes, "agency limitations, regulatory constraints and political forces" restrict rapid embrace of such technologies.[86]

It's often hard to know what we're missing because of our encrusted, bureaucratic-controlled system. "Because innovation and technological change often become apparent only after government impediments have been eliminated by policy reforms, such as privatization and deregulation, they may be difficult to identify and the costs from failing to implement them may be difficult to quantify before the policy change," the study further explains.[87]

In a somewhat philosophical 2009 book, *The Privatization of Roads and Highways,* the Mises Institute's Walter Block argues that transportation systems owned by private entities could even result in far fewer highway fatalities. Road operators would "have every incentive to try to reduce accidents, whether by technological innovations, better rules of the road, improved methods of selecting out drunken and other undesirable drivers, etc. If he failed, or did less well than his competition, he eventually would be removed from his position of responsibility."[88] We can use more of these interesting thought experiments.

Sometimes innovations exist, but governments are reluctant to implement them. The Reserve Bank study points to roughly 100,000 flights cancelled in the United States during 2014's winter season. Many businesses – including the Green Bay Packers football team – use underground heating systems to keep parking lots and sports fields snow-free. The Federal Aviation Administration deems that innovation too expensive, but the costs might be justified by more on-time departures. Its conclusion is hard to dispute: "intractable public policies have significantly compromised the performance of those public facilities."

The private sector can be remarkably creative, yet public agencies struggle to implement even long-existing technologies. In California, we expect the state to provide virtually every public service – yet the state has a history of private approaches. Following the Gold Rush, private companies built a system of 150 totally private toll roads that served not only the Sierra foothills but San Francisco and its suburbs, explained UC Irvine's Daniel Klein and Chi Yin in a 1994 *Los Angeles Times* column.[89]

They point more recently to the Orange County toll roads, which were funded by revenues rather than general taxpayer funds. In the 1970s, the county south of Los Angeles experienced remarkable population and economic growth – and ensuing traffic congestion. Local lawmakers "were unable to convince the State Highway Commission of its need for additional capacity, and only four miles of new state highway were constructed between 1975 and 1985," explained *Access* magazine.[90]

The Legislature did agree in 1987 to allow the county to create a joint-powers authority to build a series of toll roads that connected to the state highway system. The agency built four remarkable toll roads spanning 51 miles that used cutting-edge technology at the time – "automatic vehicle-identification technology, automatic toll-collection equipment, and changeable message signs to guide traffic."[91] These roads dramatically improved transportation in the southern, growing part of the county. The agency used a design-build method that kept costs under control. It even used technology to track wildlife patterns and build a sophisticated system of wildlife under-crossings.

"The Toll Roads represent a highly sustainable and stable way to finance much-needed mobility options in Southern California," the agency noted in 2018. "In fact, collectively, the annual toll revenue has grown from $41 million in 1998 to nearly $330 million in FY18."[92]

The Toll Roads have had their critics. Initially, many drivers and motorist groups objected to the idea of paying tolls on freeways. As *The Orange County Register*'s Teri Sforza explained last year, ridership and revenue predictions weren't always accurate, costs increased and the bonds have been refinanced – meaning they won't be paid off as early as predicted. Another proposed toll-road segment met with fierce opposition from affected communities. Reduced COVID ridership strained its finances.

"The toll roads were financed by bonds, which were bought by investors, and toll revenue furnishes almost all the money that repays them," Sforza wrote.[93] Critics worry that the state could be on the hook if (though highly unlikely) investors can't meet the debt payments. But they remain the most modern and functional freeways in the state. Had the county not embraced this innovative, privatized approach, what are the chances Caltrans would have built any of these roads? (Hint: ballpark zero).

Before Californians complain about a bond- and revenue-funded system that largely – though imperfectly – fulfilled its promises, they ought to look at the latest government-funded mega-transportation project, the High Speed Rail system. In 1992, then-Sen. Quentin Kopp, the San Francisco Independent who chaired the Senate Transportation Committee, introduced legislation that would lay the groundwork for a bullet train connecting the Bay Area to Los Angeles. Kopp is considered the father of the state's high-speed rail proposal.

In recent years, however, Kopp has publicly berated the rail project. "Project alterations, illegal authority and legislative acts and misrepresentations to Californians have occurred," he wrote in the *San Mateo Daily Journal* in 2021.[94] "Currently, the authority business plan provides for only one electrified track on a 119-mile route supposedly from Merced to Bakersfield."

Voters in 2008 approved Proposition 1A, which provided $9.95 billion in initial funding for the project. The initiative included many detailed promises regarding travel times, costs, budget deadlines, private investments and alignments.[95] The current proposal detours wildly from those promises. The plan's opponents filed lawsuits based on these inconsistencies, but the courts have allowed the project to move forward nonetheless. Apparently, the goal is to dig a deep enough hole, so to speak, so that there's no choice but to fill it with public dollars.

The costs have ballooned many times above original estimates. Instead of linking the state's two major metropolitan areas, the state is building a route between two smaller cities in the flat (and less challenging, from a construction standpoint) San Joaquin Valley. Private investment has not materialized. The promised 2 hour and 40 minute ride from San Francisco to Los Angeles is unlikely now that the design has the bullet train sharing tracks with commuter trains on the peninsula. It will almost certainly require operating subsidies.[96]

Even the *New York Times* recognized the project as a boondoggle. Its investigative report noted recently that, "the tortured effort to build the country's first high-speed rail system is a case study in how ambitious public works projects can become perilously encumbered by political compromise, unrealistic cost estimates, flawed engineering and a determination to persist on projects that have become, like the crippled financial institutions of 2008, too big to fail."[97]

There's nothing wrong with high-speed rail, per se. But transportation projects controlled by political and bureaucratic forces will almost certainly end up like this particular bullet-train project. By contrast, consider that a private company has proposed an $8-billion Brightline West project that might get off the ground in 2023 – record time compared to the state's bullet-train schedule. It would connect the Los Angeles suburb of Rancho Cucamonga with Las Vegas and, as *Construction Dive* reported, and "eliminate 3 million cars a year from the heavily traveled I-15 corridor."[98]

Although the states of California and Nevada will float the private activity bonds, they will be financed by private investors and will be operated by a private group with experience in Florida. Unlike the public high-speed rail project, this one conforms to obvious consumer demand.[99] Californians already have an easy way to get from the Bay Area to LA (Southwest Airlines, despite its recent problems). But it's cumbersome to take a flight or drive from Southern California to Las Vegas. Who wouldn't want to take a party train to Vegas on the weekend?

Privatization is different from truly private endeavors. With the former, government provides a franchise. These projects might be funded through revenue bonds (such as the OC toll roads), but also with direct taxpayer subsidies (as when an agency contracts with a private provider). Such approaches can improve efficiencies. I once worked at an Air Force testing facility that let the management and operation contracts out to bid every few years. That provided competitive cost constraints typically lacking in government operations. However, private franchises (such as regulated utilities) can combine the problems of monopoly contracts with the profit motive. The devil is in the contract details.

Given the complexities of building transportation systems, discussions about private-sector involvement typically involve privatization efforts. But fully private entities can and have shaken up the status quo. We all know that ridesharing companies such as Uber and Lyft transformed the ossified regulated taxi industry. Not only have those companies provided a nicer (and at times cheaper) urban riding experience, but they forced the taxi and airport shuttle industries to improve their game.

When Uber came onto the scene, taking a cab could be a miserable experience. They often lacked modern credit-card readers and it could be frustrating standing on a busy city street trying to hail a cab. I've been stuck in outer San Francisco neighborhoods repeatedly dialing 800 taxi numbers trying to convince a cab to pick me up. Lately, I've taken more taxicabs than usual because they've finally taken advantage of new technologies. They only did so, of course, because rideshare competitors forced them to improve their customer service to stay in business.

Something similar could transform the bus industry. A 2015 *Vox* article detailed emerging micro-transit companies that operate shuttle services that "occupy a middle ground between the pricey convenience of taxis and the slow, cheap service of public transit."[100] These services have yet to really take off, but it's easy to see how they – or something we've yet to envision – could improve urban transport.

And automation offers many possibilities. Although still in their infancy, self-driving cars could change the way urbanites commute. In 2021, Hamburg, Germany, unveiled an automated train system that is the product of a public-private partnership.

"With automated rail operations, we can offer our passengers a significantly expanded, more reliable and therefore improved service – without having to lay a single kilometer of new track," said the CEO of Deutsche Bahn, the German national railway company, in a statement. "It is our goal to make rail transport attractive to ever-larger numbers of people, which is the only way we can achieve the mobility transition."[101] The company says the system will serve 30 percent more customers and slash energy costs by 30 percent. German authorities apparently are serious about public transportation and understand that improving service (rather than protecting public jobs) is the paramount goal.

By contrast, American transportation planners are masters of making excuses. When it comes to freeway transportation, for instance, American transit advocates often prattle about something known as "induced demand." They argue that expanding road lanes is unnecessary because they instantly fill up anyway. "The theory of induced demand asserts that as roadways become wider and able to accommodate higher volumes of traffic, additional vehicles will materialize as drivers feel incentivized to use the expanded road due to the belief that added lanes have reduced congestion," as *Planetizen* describes it.[102]

In my view, it's not so much a serious theory as an excuse by freeway opponents to stop the construction of new lanes and interchanges. If transit systems opened new routes and the buses and trains instantly filled up with new riders, these same theorists would be ecstatic. The goal of transportation should be to facilitate people's travel, so it's hard to understand the consternation when people use new freeways and new developments spring up around them.[103]

It's not so much "induced demand" as pent-up demand. Residents who had been suffering through interminable traffic understandably drive on new roads that get them to their destinations. Research also suggests that the theory is bunk. Writing in the *Weekly Standard* in 2011, Jonathan Last pointed to research from demographer Wendell Cox suggesting the following:

> Between 1982 and 2007, Phoenix decided to build the highways it should have had in the first place. They added so much asphalt that, according to the research firm Demographia, the city's highway-lane-miles per capita grew by 205 percent. During that period, highway-vehicle-miles-traveled per capita increased by only 12 percent. And, like magic, traffic congestion plummeted.[104]

For purposes of this discussion, I'd argue that a more sensible system of paying for highways could quickly alleviate any real problems from so-called induced demand. The Orange County toll roads are heavily used but have avoided much of the grueling Southern California congestion because they, for instance, charge drivers tolls based on the mileage driven. A proper pricing mechanism is a better solution than not building road lanes. I'm not advocating for tolls or any particular solution, but merely noting that solutions exist for those who are interested in them. Then again, one would need to want to reduce congestion – rather than increase in the ill-fated hope that drivers will give up their cars and jump on transit.

Differing Visions of Modern Transportation Planning

It's pretty obvious that this Congestion Lobby is not improving urban life, but instead disrupting the lives of metropolitan residents and harming economic growth. Remarking on these urban policies that "are now voluntarily opting to slow themselves down" with Road Diets, bike lanes and whatnot, Reason Foundation's Sam Staley noted that "time spent stuck in traffic or on a slower commute or journey is time not spent shopping, eating at home with family, playing or working."[105] These are the ramifications of our misguided transportation policies.

The current transportation vision, as embraced by government planners and academics, is one where people live primarily in densely packed cities and rely on rail and buses to get around. That's why so many of their ideas involve transforming development patterns and not improving transportation nodes. To the degree that these ideas energize market forces, I'm in favor of them. Oregon has banned single-family-only zoning. California passed Senate Bills 9 and 10, which accomplish a similar result by allowing the construction of duplexes and mid-rise condominiums and apartments on a by-right basis in many single-family neighborhoods.[106] California recently passed a new law that limits the ability of localities to impose parking minimums for new projects. Those are good ideas, in that they allow private property owners to determine the "right" number of parking spots.[107]

They aren't panaceas, but they allow property owners and developers to build more projects on their own land. These up-zoning policies allow the natural market process to work by removing government impediments. If that increases density and encourages more transit use, that's fine. The government should no more mandate high-density living, however, than it should mandate low-density living. Transportation planning should meet people where they are – not where the planners want them to be.

Advocates for Transit Oriented Development often say the right things. "Transit-oriented development links transportation and land use – providing people with maximum choice in how to get around by intensifying activities near transit nodes with high quality public space," explains one article by the Congress for the New Urbanism.[108] Typically, though, this ends up meaning re-ordering land-use policies and investing the lion's share of funding in transit systems and bike lanes. New Urbanists have many useful things to say about neighborhood development, but most Americans live in the suburbs and rely on their cars. They aren't hankering to move into a downtown condo above the Quiznos.

The Free Cities Center vision is somewhat different and more practical. We have no problem with allowing higher densities, or building cost-effective transit lines that serve urbanites.

But those systems need to be vastly improved, and not just the recipients of more money to provide transit in the same-old shoddy ways. We need to unleash market forces so that new transportation options can emerge without the government's unnecessary impediments.

Transportation officials need to improve all of our transportation options, ranging from commuter rail lines to arterial streets and freeways. They need to invest in real-world solutions rather than $113-billion high-speed rail systems that serve no obvious constituency. They need to embrace technologies, outsourcing and privatization to stretch our transportation dollars, so the public that pays the bills gets the most bang for the buck. They need to put the customer first.

Fundamentally, Western states need to focus once again on civil engineering that builds quality systems that meet the public's current needs rather than social engineering designed to prod or annoy them into living in ways that the planners prefer.

Endnotes

1   Stephen Moss, "End of the car age: how cities are outgrowing the automobile," *The Guardian*, April 28, 2015, https://www.theguardian.com/cities/2015/apr/28/end-of-the-car-age-how-cities-outgrew-the-automobile

2   Bill Lindeke, "Why driving is bad for America," *Minn-Post*, August 2, 2022, https://www.minnpost.com/cityscape/2022/08/why-driving-is-bad-for-america/

3   Marcus Gee, "Pickup trucks are a plague on Canadian streets," *The Globe and Mail*, July 25, 2021, https://www.theglobeandmail.com/canada/toronto/article-pickup-trucks-are-a-plague-on-canadian-streets/

4   No More Freeways webpage, accessed Feb. 19, 2023, https://nomorefreewayspdx.com/

5   Robert Cervero, "Transforming cities with transit, UN Habitat for a Better Urban Future, accessed Feb. 19, 2023, https://unhabitat.org/transforming-cities-with-transit-robert-cervero-university-of-california-berkeley

6   Shiftan, Y., & Golani, A. (2005). Effect of Auto Re-
    straint Policies on Travel Behavior. *Transporta-
    tion Research Record, 1932*(1), 156–163. https://doi.
    org/10.1177/0361198105193200118

7   Jared Sanchez, "It's Time for California to Stop Building Free-
    ways. Full Stop." *CalBike*, July 14, 2022, https://www.calbike.
    org/california-stop-building-freeways/

8   Press Statement, "Governor Newsom Announces California
    Will Phase Out Gasoline-Powered Cars & Drastically Reduce
    Demand for Fossil Fuel in California's Fight Against Climate
    Change, Office of California Gov. Gavin Newsom, Sept. 23,
    2020, https://www.gov.ca.gov/2020/09/23/governor-new-
    som-announces-california-will-phase-out-gasoline-pow-
    ered-cars-drastically-reduce-demand-for-fossil-fuel-in-califor-
    nias-fight-against-climate-change/

9   Staff, "How evil are cars?" *Los Angeles Times*, Sept. 22, 2006,
    https://www.latimes.com/archives/la-xpm-2006-sep-22-ed-
    lockyer22-story.html

10 Gabby Birenbaum, "How to end the American obsession with
    driving," *Vox*, Sept. 15, 2021, https://www.vox.com/22662963/
    end-driving-obsession-connectivity-zoning-parking

11 Staff, "Madrid Population 2023," World Population Review,
    accessed Feb. 19, 2023, https://worldpopulationreview.com/
    world-cities/madrid-population

12 Mike Maciag, "Population Density for U.S. Cities Statistics,"
    Governing, Oct. 1, 2013, https://www.governing.com/archive/
    population-density-land-area-cities-map.html

13 Gabby Birenbaum, "How to end the American obsession with driving," *Vox*, Sept. 15, 2021, https://www.vox.com/22662963/end-driving-obsession-connectivity-zoning-parking

14 Staff, "California Transportation Plan 2050," California Department of Transportation Executive Summary, February 2021, https://dot.ca.gov/-/media/dot-media/programs/transportation-planning/documents/ctp-2050-v3-a11y.pdf

15 Ibid., p. 15

16 Press Statement, "The Bus Riders Union Makes History at the Intersection of Mass Transit, Civil Rights and the Environment," The Bus Riders Union, accessed Feb. 19, 2023, https://thestrategycenter.org/1996/09/06/new-vision/

17 Press Statement, "Bus Riders Union Motion for Free Public Transportation," accessed Feb. 19, 2023, https://thestrategycenter.org/2021/09/23/bru-motion-free-transit/

18 Alissa Walker, "L.A. Just Ran (and Ended) the Biggest Free-Transit Experiment in the U.S.," *New York*, Jan. 19, 2022, https://www.curbed.com/2022/01/los-angeles-metro-free-transit-buses.html

19 Kenneth Schrupp, "California Chooses Flashy Projects Over Quality Transit," Free Cities Center, Feb. 9, 2023, https://www.pacificresearch.org/california-chooses-flashy-projects-over-quality-transit/

20 Jonathan English, "Why Did America Give Up on Mass Transit? (Don't Blame Cars.)," *Bloomberg*, August 31, 2018, https://www.bloomberg.com/news/features/2018-08-31/why-is-american-mass-transit-so-bad-it-s-a-long-story

21 Stephen Smith, "5 Union Rules That Are Ruining Transportation," *FEE Stories*, March 12, 2017, https://fee.org/articles/5-union-rules-that-are-ruining-transportation/

22 William L. Anderson, "Mass transit in America: Pipedream or possibility?" Free Cities Center, Feb. 15, 2023, https://www.pacificresearch.org/mass-transit-in-america-pipedream-or-possibility/

23 Gwynn Guilford, "New Data Show Broad Shift to Remote Work During Pandemic," *Wall Street Journal*, Sept. 15, 2022, https://www.wsj.com/articles/new-data-show-broad-shift-to-remote-work-during-pandemic-11663214461

24 Danielle Muoio Dunn, "Transit systems across the globe face a Covid reckoning," *Politico*, Oct. 20, 2020, https://www.politico.com/states/new-york/albany/story/2020/10/20/transit-operators-across-the-globe-face-a-reckoning-1327371

25 David Schaper, "Public transit is having a slow comeback after the pandemic," NPR/KQED, Sept. 11, 2022 https://www.npr.org/2022/09/11/1122250673/public-transit-is-having-a-slow-comeback-after-the-pandemic

26 Michael Manville, Brian D. Taylor and Evelyn Blumenberg, "Falling Transit Ridership: California and Southern California," Southern California Association of Governments, January 2018, https://scag.ca.gov/sites/main/files/file-attachments/its_scag_transit_ridership.pdf

27 Ibid.

28 Staff, "Results of our 2022 Customer Experience Survey," LA Metro, Oct. 27, 2022 https://thesource.metro.net/2022/10/27/results-of-our-2022-customer-experience-survey/

29 Grace Toohey, "Women's ridership down on L.A. Metro, and satisfaction with buses, trains falls," *Los Angeles Times*, Nov. 4, 2022, https://www.latimes.com/california/story/2022-11-04/female-ridership-on-la-metro-down-satisfaction-with-county-buses-drops

30 Faiz Siddiqui, "Falling transit ridership poses an 'emergency' for cities, experts fear," *The Washington Post*, March 24, 2018, https://www.washingtonpost.com/local/trafficandcommuting/falling-transit-ridership-poses-an-emergency-for-cities-experts-fear/2018/03/20/ffb67c28-2865-11e8-874b-d517e912f125_story.html

31 Randal O'Toole, "Transit: The Urban Parasite," Cato Institute Policy Analysis, No. 889, April 20, 2020, https://www.cato.org/policy-analysis/transit-urban-parasite#introduction

32 Randal O'Toole, "Transport Costs & Subsidies by Mode," *The Anti-Planner*, Sept. 17, 2019, https://ti.org/antiplanner/?p=16441

33 Ibid.

34 Ibid.

35 Walter Block, "Public Goods and Externalities: The Case of Roads" Frasier Institute, Spring 1983, https://mises-media.s3.amazonaws.com/7_1_1_0.pdf

36 Jonathan English, "Why Did America Give Up on Mass Transit? (Don't Blame Cars.)," *Bloomberg*, August 31, 2018, https://www.bloomberg.com/news/features/2018-08-31/why-is-american-mass-transit-so-bad-it-s-a-long-story

37 Dan Wiekel, "Orange County to Decide Fate of CenterLine Project Monday," *Los Angeles Times*, July 19, 2003, https://www.latimes.com/archives/la-xpm-2003-jul-19-me-center-line19-story.html

38 Julie Leopo, "Downtown Santa Ana Merchants Demand OC Transit Agency Cushion OC Streetcar Impacts," *VoiceofOC*, July 20, 2022, https://voiceofoc.org/2022/07/downtown-san-ta-ana-merchants-demand-oc-transit-agency-cushion-oc-streetcar-impacts/

39 Joseph Stromberg, "The real reason American public transportation is such a disaster," *Vox*, Aug. 10, 2015, https://www.vox.com/2015/8/10/9118199/public-transportation-subway-buses

40 Ibid.

41 Lawrence McQuillan and Hovannes Abramyan, "Crime, Grime, and Greed at BART," Independent Institute, Jan. 19, 2022, https://www.independent.org/publications/article.asp?id=13843

42 Jason Green, "Brazen attack on BART passenger prompts calls for increased safety," *East Bay Times*, Aug. 22, 2022, https://www.eastbaytimes.com/2022/08/19/brazen-attack-on-bart-passenger-prompts-calls-for-increased-safety/

43 Lisa Fernandez, "Crime soars on BART, fare evasion costs $25M a year: grand jury report," KTVU, June 25, 2019, https://www.ktvu.com/news/violent-crime-soars-on-bart-fare-evasion-costs-25m-a-year-grand-jury-report

44 Luz Pena, "Bay Area business offers self-defense classes after recent public transit attacks," ABC7 News, Jan. 19, 2023, https://abc7news.com/bart-attack-muni-sf-self-defense-class-public-transit/12717375/

45 Ed West, "Did cars kill urban life?" Wrong Side of History by Ed West, Substack, Oct. 19, 2022, https://edwest.substack.com/p/did-cars-kill-urban-life

46 Press Statement, "President Biden, USDOT Announce More than $20 Billion for Communities of All Sizes to Support Transit This Year, Federal Transit Administration, April 6, 2022, https://www.transit.dot.gov/about/news/president-biden-usdot-announce-more-20-billion-communities-all-sizes-support-transit

47 Press Statement, "Governor Newsom Announces Awards of $2.5 Billion for Public Transportation Projects Throughout California," Office of Gov. Gavin Newsom, Jan. 31, 2023, https://www.gov.ca.gov/2023/01/31/governor-newsom-announces-awards-of-2-5-billion-for-public-transportation-projects-throughout-california/

48 Lawrence McQuillan and Hovannes Abramyan, "Crime, Grime, and Greed at BART," Independent Institute, Jan. 19, 2022, https://www.independent.org/publications/article.asp?id=13843

49 Transparent California is a database of public pay and pensions: https://transparentcalifornia.com/

50 Staff, "Strikes over pensions to disrupt public transport in France on Tuesday," *Reuters*, Jan. 29, 2023, https://www.reuters.com/world/europe/strikes-will-disrupt-public-transport-france-tuesday-minister-says-2023-01-29/

51 Steven Greenhut, "Bus drivers should thank OCTA management," *The Orange County Register*, July 17, 2007, https://www.ocregister.com/2007/07/17/bus-drivers-should-thank-octa-management/

52 Tori Richards, "California seeks to curtail freeway expansion because it's 'racist' and not green," *Washington Examiner*, April 20, 2022, https://www.washingtonexaminer.com/restoring-america/equality-not-elitism/california-seeks-to-curtail-freeway-expansion-citing-racism-and-environment

53 Melanie Curry, "No-Freeway-Expansion Bill Dies in Senate Committee," Streets Blog Cal, June 29, 2022, https://cal.streetsblog.org/2022/06/29/no-freeway-expansion-bill-dies-in-senate-committee/

54 Assembly Bill 1778, California Legislative Information, Assembly Floor Analysis, May 20, 2022, https://leginfo.legislature.ca.gov/faces/billNavClient.xhtml?bill_id=202120220AB1778

55 Steven Greenhut, *Back From Dystopia: A New Vision for Western Cities*, Pacific Research Institute, Sept. 123, 2022, https://www.amazon.com/Back-Dystopia-Vision-Western-Cities/dp/1934276480

56 Anthony Paletta, "Story of cities #32: Jane Jacobs v Robert Moses, battle of New York's urban titans," *The Guardian*, April 28, 2016, https://www.theguardian.com/cities/2016/apr/28/story-cities-32-new-york-jane-jacobs-robert-moses

57 Claire Wang, "Federal Highway Removal Program Raises Hopes in California," *The American Prospect*, May 16, 2022, https://prospect.org/infrastructure/building-back-america/federal-highway-removal-program-raises-hopes-in-california/

58 James Sterngold, "California Governor Sees an End to Freeway Building," *The New York Times*, Aug. 21, 2001, https://www.nytimes.com/2001/08/21/us/california-governor-sees-an-end-to-freeway-building.html

59 Staff, "California Transportation Plan 2050," California Department of Transportation Executive Summary, February 2021, https://dot.ca.gov/-/media/dot-media/programs/transportation-planning/documents/ctp-2050-v3-a11y.pdf

60 Wendell Cox, "Cars: Principal Mobility for Workers in Poverty," *New Geography*, Dec. 23, 2017, https://www.newgeography.com/content/005832-cars-principal-mobility-workers-povertyz

61 Wendell Cox, "Planners push transit, but it's a hard sell in Western cities," Free Cities Center, Nov. 10, 2022, https://www.pacificresearch.org/planners-push-transit-but-its-a-hard-sell-in-western-cities/

62 Ibid.

63 Ibid.

64 Scott Beyer, "How Cars, Not Subways, Will Make Us Richer," *The Daily Beast*, June 4, 2014, http://www.thedailybeast.com/articles/2014/06/04/how-cars-not-subways-will-make-us-richer.html

65 Senate Bill 1, California Legislative Information, Assembly Floor Analysis, April 6, 2017, https://leginfo.legislature.ca.gov/faces/billNavClient.xhtml?bill_id=201720180SB1

66 Jon Coupal, "The great gas tax rip-off continues," *The Daily Breeze*, April 18, 2021, https://www.dailybreeze.com/2021/04/18/the-great-gas-tax-ripoff-continues/

67 Christopher LeGras, "From Los Angeles to Washington, DC, 'road diets' threaten local businesses," Better Cities Project, Sept. 12, 2019, https://better-cities.org/transportation-infrastructure/from-los-angeles-to-washington-road-diets-threaten-businesses/

68 Ibid.

69 Staff, "Road Diets (Roadway Reconfiguration)," U.S. Federal Highway Administration, accessed Feb. 19, 2023, https://highways.dot.gov/safety/other/road-diets

70 Andrew Keatts, "What Are 'Road Diets,' and Why Are They Controversial?" Rice University Kinder Institute for Urban Research, Sept. 10, 2015, https://kinder.rice.edu/urbanedge/what-are-road-diets-and-why-are-they-controversial

71 Patrick McGreevy, "Gas tax pays for slimmer streets," *Los Angeles Times*, Oct. 31, 2017, https://enewspaper.latimes.com/infinity/article_share.aspx?guid=5536ff4e-344a-42d7-887d-4ff009e1863e

72 Sheila Dunn, "The Problem with Road Diets," National Motorists Association, Feb. 16, 2018, https://ww2.motorists.org/blog/problem-road-diets/

73 Samuel Speroni, Asha Weinstein Agrawai PhD., Michael Manville PhD., et. al, "Charging Drivers by the Gallon vs. the Mile: An Equity Analysis by Geography and Income in California," San Jose State University, September 2022, https://transweb.sjsu.edu/research/2238-Equity-Analysis-Road-User-Charge

74 Elaine Povitch, "As Electric Vehicles Shrink Gas Tax Revenue, More States May Tax Mileage," *Stateline*, Oct. 10, 2022, https://www.pewtrusts.org/en/research-and-analysis/blogs/stateline/2022/10/10/as-electric-vehicles-shrink-gas-tax-revenue-more-states-may-tax-mileage

75 Willie Brown, "When Warriors travel to China, Ed Lee will follow," *San Francisco Chronicle*, July 27, 2013, https://www.sfchronicle.com/bayarea/williesworld/article/When-Warriors-travel-to-China-Ed-Lee-will-follow-4691101.php

76   Joe Gose, "'The Grand Central Station Of The West': Giant Transit Hub In San Francisco Opens," *Forbes*, Aug. 14, 2018, https://www.forbes.com/sites/joegose/2018/08/14/giant-transit-hub-aims-to-enhance-economic-vitality-south-of-market/?sh=3eebfa705c63

77   LeBlanc, Steve, "On December 31, It's Official: Boston's Big Dig Will Be Done," *The Washington Post,* Dec. 26, 2007, https://www.washingtonpost.com/wp-dyn/content/article/2007/12/25/AR2007122500600.html

78   Danielle Torrent Tucker, "Q&A: 30 years after the Loma Prieta earthquake," *Stanford Earth Matters*, Oct. 16, 2019, https://earth.stanford.edu/news/qa-30-years-after-loma-prieta-earthquake

79   Eric Jaffe, "From $250 Million to $6.5 Billion: The Bay Bridge Cost Overrun," *CityLab*, Oct. 13, 2015, https://www.bloomberg.com/news/articles/2015-10-13/how-the-cost-of-remaking-the-san-francisco-bay-bridge-soared-to-6-5-billion

80   Abdulelah Aljohani, Dominic Ahiaga-Dagbui, and David Moore, "Construction Projects Cost Overrun: What Does the Literature Tell Us?" *International Journal of Innovation, Management and Technology*, Vol. 8, No. 2, April 2017, http://www.ijimt.org/vol8/717-MP0022.pdf

81   Joseph S. Szyliowicz, "The private sector is the answer to America's huge transportation infrastructure problem," *Quartz*, Sept. 1, 2015, https://qz.com/491726/the-private-sector-is-the-answer-to-americas-huge-transportation-infrastructure-problem

82   Baruch Feigenbaum and Spence Purnell, "Annual Highway Report: Ranking each state's highway conditions and cost-effectiveness," Reason Foundation, Nov. 18, 2021, https://reason.org/policy-study/26th-annual-highway-report/

83 Mac Taylor, "The 2014-15 Budget: Capital Outlay Support Program Review, Legislative Analyst's Office, May 14, 2014, https://lao.ca.gov/reports/2014/budget/capital-outlay/capital-outlay-support-program-051414.pdf

84 Katrina Schwartz, "End of an Era: No More Toll Takers on Bay Area Bridges," KQED, April 8, 2021, https://www.kqed.org/news/11868435/end-of-an-era-no-more-toll-takers-on-bay-area-bridges

85 Clifford Winston, "How the Private Sector Can Improve Public Transportation Infrastructure," Research Summary, Mercatus Center at George Mason University, June 17, 2014, https://www.mercatus.org/research/working-papers/how-private-sector-can-improve-public-transportation-infrastructure#:~:text=privatization%20that%20converts%20provision%20of,provision%20of%20roads%20and%20airports

86 Ibid.

87 Ibid.

88 Walter Block, "The Privatization of Roads and Highways: Human and Economic Factors," Ludwig von Mises Institute, 2009, p.15, https://mises.org/library/privatization-roads-and-highways

89 Daniel B. Klein and Chi Yin, "ORANGE COUNTY VOICES: History Holds Lesson in Toll Road Success," *Los Angeles Times*, June 6, 1994, https://www.latimes.com/archives/la-xpm-1994-06-06-me-911-story.html

90 Gordon Fielding, "Investigating Toll Roads in California," *Access*, 1992, https://www.accessmagazine.org/spring-1993/investigating-toll-roads-in-california/

91   Ibid.

92   Press Statement, "Celebrating 20 Years of Keeping People Moving in Southern California," The Toll Roads of Orange County, Nov. 18, 2018, https://thetollroads.com/news/newsroom/celebrating-20-years-of-keeping-people-moving-in-southern-california/

93   Teri Sforza, "Toll roads' traffic, revenue took big hit in OC during pandemic," *The Orange County Register*, Oct. 20, 2022, https://www.ocregister.com/2022/10/20/toll-roads-traffic-revenue-took-big-hit-in-oc-during-pandemic/

94   Quentin L. Kopp, "High-speed rail subterfuge," *San Mateo Daily Journal*, March 29, 2021, https://www.smdailyjournal.com/opinion/guest_perspectives/high-speed-rail-subterfuge/article_a3809f86-903d-11eb-b80b-5f24baba8ed6.html

95   California Proposition 1A, Ballotpedia, https://ballotpedia.org/California_Proposition_1A,_High-Speed_Rail_Bond_Measure_(2008), accessed Feb. 20, 2023

96   Matt Welch, "We Told You Why and How California's High-Speed Rail Wouldn't Work. You Chose Not To Listen," *Reason*, Oct. 13, 2022, https://reason.com/2022/10/13/we-told-you-why-and-how-californias-high-speed-rail-wouldnt-work-you-chose-not-to-listen/

97   Ralph Vartabedian, "How California's Bullet Train Went Off the Rails," *The New York Times*, Oct. 9, 2022, https://www.nytimes.com/2022/10/09/us/california-high-speed-rail-politics.html

98 Dan Zukowski, "High-speed rail line from LA to Las Vegas could begin construction in 2023," *Construction Dive*, Dec. 5, 2022, https://www.constructiondive.com/news/high-speed-rail-construction-los-angeles-las-vegas-Brightline/637945/

99 Ibid.

100 Joseph Stromberg, "These startups want to do for buses what Uber did for taxi rides," *Vox*, July 7, 2015, https://www.vox.com/2015/7/7/8906027/microtransit-uber-buses

101 Kristin Houser, "Germany unveils first-of-its-kind autonomous train," *Free Think*, Oct. 16, 2021, https://www.freethink.com/hard-tech/autonomous-train

102 Staff, "What is Induced Demand?" *Planetizen*, https://www.planetizen.com/definition/induced-demand, accessed Feb. 20, 2023

103 Matthew Yglesias, "What does 'induced demand' really amount to?" *Slow Boring*, Jan. 17, 2023, https://www.slowboring.com/p/what-does-induced-demand-really-amount

104 Jonathan V. Last, "More Highways, Less Congestion," *Weekly Standard*, March 7, 2011, https://www.texasturf.org/2012-06-01-03-09-30/latest-news/1508-theory-of-induced-travel-debunked

105 Samuel Staley, "Traffic Congestion and the Economic Decline of Cities," Reason Foundation, Jan. 5, 2012, https://reason.org/commentary/traffic-congestion-and-the-economic/

106 Steven Greenhut, "Land-use bill promotes freedom and property rights," *The Orange County Register*, Aug. 27, 2021, https://www.ocregister.com/2021/08/27/land-use-bill-promotes-freedom-and-property-rights/

107 Christian Britschgi, "Cities Switch From Requiring Too Many Parking Spaces to Banning Too Many Parking Spaces," *Reason*, Nov. 22, 2022, https://reason.com/2022/11/22/cities-switch-from-requiring-too-many-parking-spaces-to-banning-too-many-parking-spaces/

108 Robert Steuteville, "Great idea: Transit-oriented development," *Public Square: A CNU Journal*, March 15, 2017, https://www.cnu.org/publicsquare/2017/03/15/great-idea-transit-oriented-development

About the Author

STEVEN GREENHUT is a longtime journalist who has covered California politics since 1998. He wrote this book for the San Francisco-based Pacific Research Institute, where he founded that think tank's Sacramento-based journalism center in 2009. He currently is western region director for the R Street Institute, a Washington, D.C.-based free-market think tank, and is on the editorial board of the Southern California News Group. Greenhut has worked fulltime as a columnist for the *Orange County Register* and the *San Diego Union-Tribune*. He writes weekly for *American Spectator* and *Reason* magazines. He is the editor of *Saving California,* and the author of *Winning the Water Wars, Abuse of Power* and *Plunder.* He also is author of PRI's 2022 book, *Back from Dystopia: A New Vision for Western Cities.* He lives with his wife, Donna, on an acreage outside Sacramento and has three adult daughters.

About Pacific Research Institute

The Pacific Research Institute (PRI) champions freedom, opportunity, and personal responsibility by advancing free-market policy solutions. It provides practical solutions for the policy issues that impact the daily lives of all Americans, and demonstrates why the free market is more effective than the government at providing the important results we all seek: good schools, quality health care, a clean environment, and a robust economy.

Founded in 1979 and based in San Francisco, PRI is a non-profit, non-partisan organization supported by private contributions. Its activities include publications, public events, media commentary, community leadership, legislative testimony, and academic outreach.

Center for Business and Economics

PRI shows how the entrepreneurial spirit—the engine of economic growth and opportunity—is stifled by onerous taxes, regulations, and lawsuits. It advances policy reforms that promote a robust economy, consumer choice, and innovation.

Center for Education

PRI works to restore to all parents the basic right to choose the best educational opportunities for their children. Through research and grassroots outreach, PRI promotes parental choice in education, high academic standards, teacher quality, charter schools, and school-finance reform.

Center for the Environment

PRI reveals the dramatic and long-term trend toward a cleaner, healthier environment. It also examines and promotes the essential ingredients for abundant resources and environmental quality: property rights, markets, local action, and private initiative.

Center for Health Care

PRI demonstrates why a single-payer Canadian model would be detrimental to the health care of all Americans. It proposes market-based reforms that would improve affordability, access, quality, and consumer choice.

Center for California Reform

The Center for California Reform seeks to reinvigorate California's entrepreneurial self-reliant traditions. It champions solutions in education, business, and the environment that work to advance prosperity and opportunity for all the state's residents.

Center for Medical Economics and Innovation

The Center for Medical Economics and Innovation aims to educate policymakers, regulators, health care professionals, the media, and the public on the critical role that new technologies play in improving health and accelerating economic growth.

Free Cities Center

The Free Cities Center cultivates innovative ideas to improve our cities and urban life based around freedom and property rights – not government.

www.ingramcontent.com/pod-product-compliance
Lightning Source LLC
Chambersburg PA
CBHW070029030426
42335CB00017B/2355